D1528543

MINI ANIMALS

Dexter Cattle

by Alix Wood

WINDMILL
BOOKS

New York

Published in 2017 by **Windmill Books**, An Imprint of Rosen Publishing
29 East 21st Street, New York, NY 10010

Editor: Eloise Macgregor
Designer: Alix Wood
Consultant: David Jones, lifetime Member of the American Dexter Cattle Association

Photo Credits: Cover, 1, 6 right, 10, 12, 22, 25 © AdobeStock; 4-5, 17, 28 © David Jones; 6 left © DollarPhotoClub; Szvivi/Dreamstime; 8, 9 top left, 14, 19 © Colin Williams; 9 top right and bottom © Mudchute Park and Farm; 11 © Joseph and Jade Lewis; 13, 16, 21 © Dreamstime; 15, 23 © Henry Williams; 18, 29 © Shutterstock; 20 © Linda & Mark Riederer at Little Bo Farm; 24 © apCincy/iStock; 26 © Joe, Rebecca, Hayden & Kaitlyn Gygax at Maple Hill Dexters; 27 © John Martin/Alamy

Cataloging-in-Publication Data
Names: Wood, Alix.
Title: Dexter cattle / Alix Wood.
Description: New York : Windmill Books, 2017. | Series: Mini animals| Includes index.
Identifiers: ISBN 9781499481525 (pbk.) | ISBN 9781499481532 (library bound) |
    ISBN 9781508192954 (6 pack)
Subjects: LCSH: Cows--Juvenile literature. | Cattle--Juvenile literature.
Classification: LCC SF197.5 W66 2017 | DDC 636.2--dc23

Manufactured in the United States of America
CPSIA Compliance Information: Batch #: BW17PK. For Further Information contact: Windmill Books, New York, New York at 1-866-478-0556

3CPLI00019329H

Contents

Tiny Dexter Cattle 4

Where Are Dexters From?...................6

Short Legs and Long Legs.........................8

The Ideal House Cow 10

Caring for a Dexter.................................12

Getting to Know a Dexter 14

Baby Dexters 16

Dexter Bulls...18

Good Mothers..20

Little Milkers 22

Working Dexters.......................................24

At the Showground.................................26

Test Your Knowledge 28

Glossary 30

Further Information.................................31

Index and Answers.................................32

Tiny Dexter Cattle

Dexters are a very small breed of cattle. They are around the same size as a tiny Shetland pony. Dexters are half the height of some larger breeds of cattle. They can be either black, red, or **dun**-colored.

Cute little Dexters were once a **rare** breed but recently they have become more popular. Their small size means they are easy to handle, and need less **pasture** than larger cattle. They are happy in hot or cold climates, and can live outdoors all year round if they have some shelter. People keep Dexters as pets, for their milk, and for their meat.

Cute Alert!

This tiny Dexter **calf** would be hidden if it laid down in the wild flowers. Dexter mothers often hide their calves in long grass to keep them safe.

5

Where Are Dexters From?

Dexter cattle originally came from the south and southwest region of Ireland. The area is rocky and mountainous and has very little shelter. Because of this and the lack of good grazing, only the smaller, **hardier** animals survived. Gradually, the breed developed into the little Dexters we know today.

Ireland

Great
Britain

The rugged Irish coastline is a harsh place for animals to live. Not much grass grows on the rocky soil.

Dexters became known in Ireland as the "poor man's cow." They needed less food and less space than larger breeds of cattle. This made them perfect for the farmers who didn't have a lot of pasture. Farmers would not even need to build them a barn. Because they are hardy animals, in a mild climate like Ireland's they would have been able to spend all their time outdoors.

Cute Alert!

Cows don't have any front top teeth. To graze, they us their bottom teeth, their top gums, and their tongues to pull grass into their mouths.

Short Legs and Long Legs

Some Dexter cattle have a form of **dwarfism**, which means that their legs are a little shorter than regular Dexters. Some short-legged Dexters do not have dwarfism, though, just short legs!

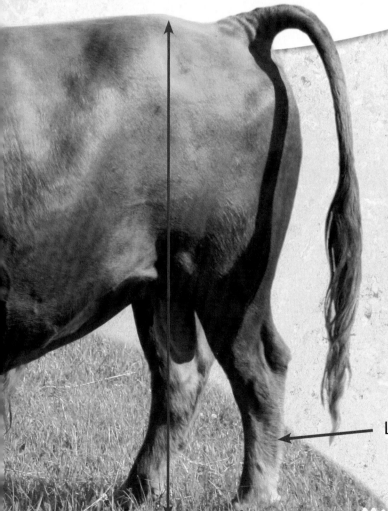

Dexters are usually measured from the hip. **Bulls** are usually between 36-50 inches (91-127 cm) tall. **Cows** are usually between 34-46 inches (86-117 cm) tall. Dexters continue to grow until they are 5 or 6 years old.

Long-legged Dexter

Long-legged Dexter   Short-legged Dexter

Short-legged Dexters are typically around 20 percent shorter than a regular Dexter. They can be a little **stockier**, too.

Short-legged Dexters with dwarfism are perfectly healthy. However, if a short-legged Dexter is bred with another short-legged animal, their young may not survive.

Cute Alert!

Only the lower halves of a short-legged Dexter's legs are shorter. Their other leg bones are the same length as a long-legged Dexter.

The Ideal House Cow

Dexters make the perfect house cow. The term "house cow" doesn't mean that the cow lives indoors though! Years ago, many people living in the countryside would keep a milking cow to provide their family with fresh milk. That animal was known as a house cow.

Because of their friendly nature, some owners take their Dexters to visit hospitals or nursing homes to cheer up the people there.

This Dexter is happy to be stroked while he is lying on the grass.

Their small size means Dexters are quite easy to keep and are gentle with children. They make great pets. They look cute and have great personalities. The cattle are also favorites with petting zoos for the same reasons.

Caring for a Dexter

Even though Dexters are small, they still need around an acre of good pasture each to graze. They'll also need a small shelter. Cattle are **herd** animals, so it is best to keep more than one, or they get lonely.

If grass is poor, Dexters will need extra food such as hay. They also need **mineral** blocks to lick. The blocks add minerals to the cattle's diet that may be missing from the local grass.

mineral block

Cute Alert!

Dexters, like most cattle, will often lick people's hands. Humans sweat salt, so to them you are just another salt lick!

Dexters need plenty of fresh water to drink. Cattle drink a lot of water. Each Dexter will need around 20 gallons (91 liters) a day.

ear tag

Dexter cattle are farm animals. In most countries, owners are required to keep records of their animals. Each animal will usually be given an identity number which is put on an ear tag. Other information, such as what **vaccinations** the animal has had, can also be put onto ear tags.

Getting to Know a Dexter

If you decide to keep Dexters, you will need to spend time building a bond with them. Spending just a few minutes a day gently grooming your Dexter will eventually earn their trust. Grooming time is also a useful way to check over an animal for any illness or injury.

Like humans, cattle form close friendships and will often choose to spend time with one or two of their close cattle friends. They also may dislike certain herd members. Cows produce more milk when they are treated well and are happy.

How to Groom a Dexter

1. Start by brushing out any dead hair and dried-on mud using a shedding comb. Use an upward motion, moving toward the head.

2. Gently wet the coat with a hose. Avoid the eyes and ears. Wash the Dexter with a bucket of cattle soap and water. Don't use soap more than once a week as it will dry out the coat.

3. Using a damp cloth, gently wash around the eyes, nose, and ears.

4. Scrub the coat using a stiff brush. Brush in circular motions. Scrub around the Dexter's hooves. Be careful in case the animal kicks.

5. Gently untangle the tail hair using a tail comb. If it is very tangled, use some conditioner.

shedding comb

stiff brush

tail comb

Baby Dexters

Little Dexter calves are very cute. They are very determined, too. They can usually get to their feet minutes after being born. They have a strong bond with their mother.

Cute Alert!

This Dexter mother is staying close to her calf. New mothers can get pretty tired having to follow their calves as they run around exploring!

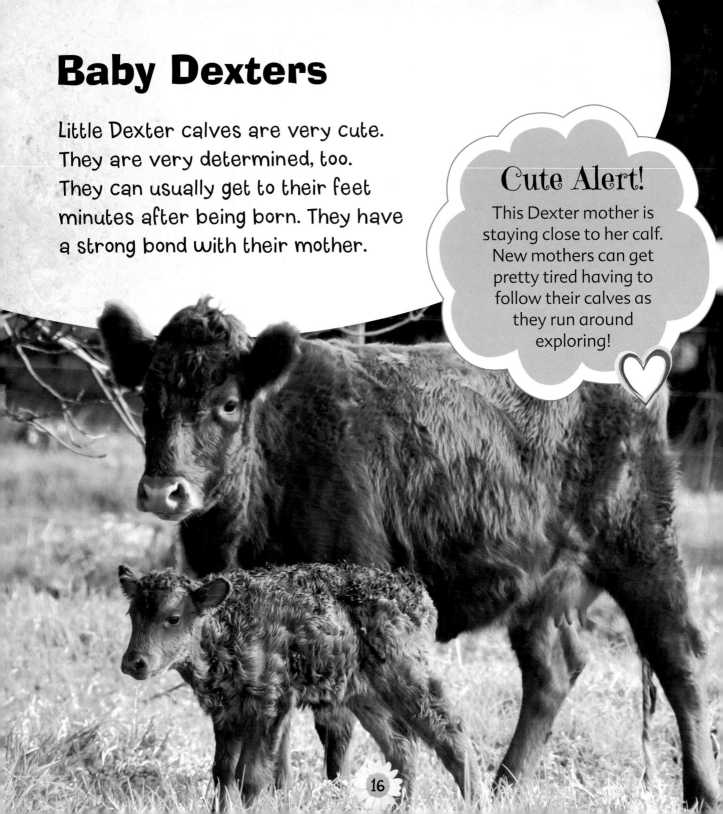

Dexters, like all cattle, are **mammals**. That means that their young drink milk produced by the mother. Some bold young Dexters will even drink milk from a cow that isn't their mother! The cows don't seem to mind.

This calf is red. Though Dexters can be black, red, or dun, most are black. A black mother can have a red calf if both she and the calf's father have red in their family.

Dexter Bulls

Bulls can be pretty big and frightening. A bull from a large breed of cattle can be as tall as an average man. Dexter bulls only grow to around the same height as an eight-year-old child. They are usually friendly, too. Even friendly bulls can be a handful though. Some owners **dehorn** their bulls, as they sometimes push using their heads, even if it's just to get attention.

Bulls need to be treated kindly but firmly. It's a good idea not to turn your back on a bull just in case!

For safety, many agricultural show organizers ask that bulls have a nose ring. The ring is put through a soft area of skin at the front of the bull's nose. The rings are usually placed on the bull when they are around 12 months old. It is usually done by a **veterinarian**. Handlers can then train their bull to move by giving a gentle tug on the ring, and then guide the bull using a halter.

Cute Alert!

There's an old saying that when you ring a bull, make sure you are not around to watch. He will never forget, or forgive whoever was there!

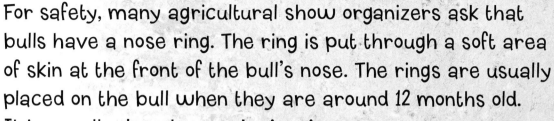

Good Mothers

Dexter cows carry their young for nine months, just like humans do. They usually have their calves without any need for a vet's help. Dexter cows are great at looking after their young. They will produce enough milk to feed two or three calves. Sometimes they feed calves that are not even theirs!

Cows naturally protect their calves. A cow protecting her young is much more dangerous than any bull. This little calf will be very safe next to mom.

Cute Alert!

Dexters will sometimes feed their calves until they are around one year old. This feeding calf is almost as big as its mother!

Dexter calves usually stop drinking their mother's milk at around seven months old. On their diet of rich milk, the calves grow to about eight times the size they were when they were born! Calves stop growing at around five or six years old. Dexter cows live for around 20 years, and can have many calves.

Little Milkers

People that own Dexter cattle often keep them for their milk. Dexters' milk is very good-quality, rich milk that is high in **butterfat**. Dexters typically produce about half the milk as a large dairy breed but it is easily enough for a family and the calf.

Cute Alert!

Milking is a chore. It must be done twice a day. You can milk a Dexter just once a day and let her calf have the rest of the milk. It makes life much nicer for everyone!

Making Butter from Dexter Milk

1. Put your milk in a clear container in the refrigerator for a couple of days. Skim off the cream from the top and put it in a jar with a lid.

2. Shake the jar until the butter separates from the buttermilk. You can use a mixer or blender instead of shaking by hand. As the butter starts to form, shake or mix more slowly.

3. Pour off the buttermilk. Wrap the butter in **muslin**. Dip the wrapped butter in a bowl of iced water. Replace the water and repeat until the water stays clear.

4. Knead the butter with a wooden spoon and add a little salt. Press the butter into a container. It is now ready to use.

People use their Dexter's milk for several different things. They might drink it, or make butter, cream, or cheese from it.

You can make a simple soft cheese by adding a pinch of salt and a few squirts of lemon juice to some fresh milk. The lemon juice causes lumps to form in the milk. Strain away the leftover liquid using a muslin and press the lumps together.

Working Dexters

Some people use Dexters as **oxen**. Oxen are working cattle that can be used to pull plows and wagons, or haul firewood. Dexters are surprisingly strong. Oxen are usually male animals because they are larger and stronger than the females. Two oxen are normally used together in a pair, known as a "team" or "span."

It takes time to train a team of oxen. An ox driver usually uses voice commands to control his team. The oxen learn six commands: forward, left, right, back, back right, and back left. Drivers may use different words for these commands.

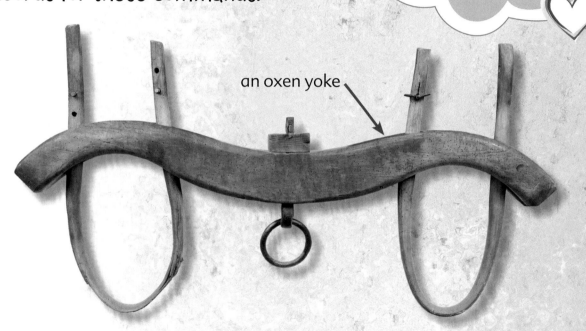

an oxen yoke

Oxen wear a yoke around their necks which attaches to whatever they are pulling. The Dexters' horns keep their heads from being able to slip out.

The oxen raise their heads and press their horns against the yoke to help brake when going down hills.

At the Showground

Part of the fun of keeping cattle is taking them to local livestock shows. There's a lot to do to get ready for a show. Dexters must be washed and groomed to look their best. **Handlers** also need to practice leading their Dexter, and to get them used to the buzz of the show-ring.

Young handlers and their cattle can win ribbons in the ring. There are lots of different classes to enter.

Cute Alert!

The show-ring can be frightening for the cattle. Handlers need to be patient. It takes a while just to get their Dexter used to wearing a halter.

To lead a Dexter, handlers hold the leading rein loosely, and gently encourage the Dexter forward. To move backward, they press the Dexter's shoulder gently using their fingertips. It is dangerous to put fingers through the halter's ring, or wrap the lead rein around a hand or wrist.

Test Your Knowledge

1. Which of these colors can a Dexter be?
   a) blue b) dun c) green

2. Where did Dexters originally come from?
   a) Ireland b) Denmark c) Canada

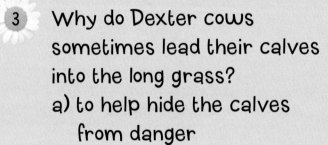

3. Why do Dexter cows sometimes lead their calves into the long grass?
   a) to help hide the calves from danger
   b) because long grass is tasty
   c) to keep them cool

4. Which of these is a type of Dexter?
   a) short-eared
   b) long-nosed
   c) short-legged

5 What is a house cow?
  a) a cow that likes to live indoors
  b) a cow kept for milk by a family
  c) a cow as big as a house

6 How long do Dexter cows carry their young?
  a) nine months b) a year
  c) three days

7 What is the best way to lead a Dexter using a harness?
  a) put your finger through the metal ring and pull
  b) wrap the lead rein around your wrist and pull
  c) hold the lead rein in your hand and guide the Dexter

8 What does an oxen wear to help him pull a plow?
  a) a joke b) a yoke c) a poke

How did you do? The answers are on page 32.

Glossary

bulls Adult male cattle.

butterfat The natural fat in milk.

calf The young of the domestic cow.

cows Adult female cattle.

dehorn To remove the horns from an animal.

dun A slightly brownish dark gray color.

dwarfism Short stature that results from a genetic condition.

handlers People in charge of an animal.

hardier More capable of coping with difficult conditions.

herd A number of animals of one kind living together.

mammals Warm-blooded animals that have a backbone and hair, breathe air, and feed milk to their young.

mineral A naturally occurring substance such as salt, usually in the form of crystals.

muslin A cotton woven fabric often used for straining liquid.

oxen Working cattle.

pasture Land used for grazing.

rare Uncommon.

stockier More thickset.

vaccinations Injections that keep an animal from getting a particular disease.

veterinarian A person who treats diseases and injuries of animals.

Further Information

Books

Caldwell, Charlotte. *The Cow's Girl:*
The Making of a Real Cowgirl.
Clyde Park, MT : Barn Board Press, 2015.

Doyle, Sheri. *Cows (Farm Animals).* North
Mankato, MN: Raintree, 2016

Murray, Julie. *Cows (Farm Animals).*
Edina, MN: Abdo Kids, 2015.

Websites

For web resources related to the
subject of this book, go to:
www.windmillbooks.com/weblinks
and select this book's title.

Index

B

bulls 8, 18, 19

butter 23

C

calves 5, 16, 17, 20, 21, 22

cheese 23

cows 5, 8, 16, 17, 20, 21

D

dehorning 18

dwarfism 8, 9

G

grazing 6, 7

grooming 14, 15

H

house cows 10

I

Ireland 6, 7

L

long-legged Dexters 8, 9

M

milk 4, 10, 14, 17, 20, 21, 22, 23

mineral licks 12

N

nose rings 19

O

oxen 24, 25

S

short-legged Dexters 8, 9

showing Dexters 26, 27

V

vaccinations 13

Answers 1) b, 2) a, 3) a, 4) c, 5) b, 6) a, 7) c, 8) b